Joyful Noise

for three or more voices

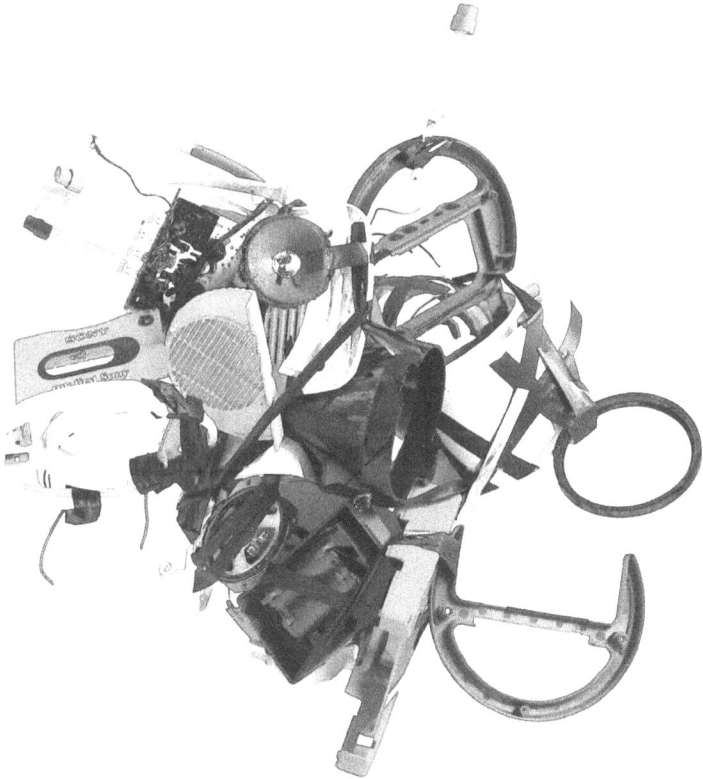

Mathew Timmons

Joyful Noise

for three or more voices

Mathew Timmons

Jaded Ibis Press
sustainable literature by digital means.™
an imprint of Jaded Ibis Productions U.S.A.

© 2012 copyright Mathew Timmons

First edition. All rights reserved.

ISBN-13: 978-1-937543-01-3
Library of Congress Control Number: 2012931372

Printed in the United States of America. No part of this book may be used or reproduced in any manner whatsoever without written permission from the publisher, except in the case of brief quotations embodied in critical articles and reviews. For information please email: questions@ jadedibisproductions.com

Published by Jaded Ibis Press, *sustainable literature by digital means*™ An imprint of Jaded Ibis Productions, LLC, Seattle, Washington USA jadedibisproductions.com

Art by Joshua Callaghan. Front Cover: "My First Sony TCM-4500 Cassette Player and Black and Decker Cafe Noir Coffee maker, modified - Does Not Make Coffee or Play Cassettes." Back Cover: "Mr. Coffee ARX32, modified - Does Not Make Coffee"

Cover design by Mathew Timmons

This book is also available in digital and fine art limited editions. Visit our website for more information.

"The lips of truth shall be established forever…
A lying tongue is but for a moment, ephemeral."

– Proverbs 12:19

ACKNOWLEDGEMENTS

The author would like to thank: Harold Abramowitz, Joshua Callaghan, Allison Carter, Corey Fogel, Ben Rodkin, Sam Witt and Jaded Ibis Press.

An earlier version of the first section, *Lip Service*, was published as a chapbook by Slack Buddha Press in February 2009.

An earlier version of the second section, *Sound Noise*, was published as a Lulu project e-edition by Little Red Leaves in September 2010.

The following pieces appeared previously: "At breakfast," "Yes, the whole idea," "Noise canceling," and "As I have reported" in *Aufgabe* Number Ten, 2011. "Every week," "I dunno," "First, you want," "Martin Luther King Jr.," and "As the angels" in *[out of nothing]* #3 [*... that there were some ah-ness to things]* 2010. "A witness to evil," "Advocating for conservation," "I couldn't help," "Apparently, what we thought," "I glared at you," and "Personal Wealth Advice" translated into Spanish in *Luvina 57* | Los Angeles City, 2010. "Why am I silent," "They say your abilities," "It's safe to assume," "My it felt like torture," and "You know how" in *Area Sneaks*, Issue #2, 2009. Part I. from the final section, *Basic Hearing on Poeticanet*, 2009. "Power trippers," "No, my opinion," "I want to buy," and "You may either" in *Try*, November 2008. "If I cover" in *Corduroy Mtn.*, November 2008. "Speak Slowly," and "Unspoken Fiction" in *moonlit* no. 3, 2008. "V for Vixen," "A Glimpse into the Secret Insides," "No Pain, No Gain," and "Attractive Attributes" in *Nod* issue number 8, 2008. "Big Muscles, Big Bodies, Big Trouble," "Pepper and Salt," "Oral Exams," "Tease Me Baby!" "Speak Slowly," "Try It, You'll Like It," and "Sleep Surgery," in *PRECIPICe* Vol. 16, Issue 1, 2008. "The good thing," "Now, you may," "I felt you," "After having made," "When you got up," and "Is it my place" in *Or*, Issue #1, 2008.

CONTENTS

I.   Lip Service   9

II.   Sound Noise   31

III.   Basic Hearing   73

A Note On Process   115

I. Lip Service

Mathew Timmons

Think Before You Speak

Lying lips are dealing
abomination to the Eternal,
but that they kneel down
with their descendants around

while smoking is directly
linked to the mouth,
itself all lips, tongue, throat,
voicebox, gullet, kidney, bladder,
pancreas, stomach and gall.

Some pharyngeal consonants
if just sipped would
produce a burning of the lips,
and also if swallowed,
destroy the muscles in the cheek.

Use a mirror to look inside
your mouth, including the roof,
cheeks, lips, gums
and under the tongue.

Examine for any white or red
spot that stands out. My tongue
was licking it while my lips
were completely inside my mouth

and then releasing it, to start again.

Speak Slowly

Of face, lips, tongue
prescription, bin, icon
a cheap throat occurrence.

An order for tongue
or throat occurs.
Lips, tongue, a cheap throat and
calls for medical attention.

Shove your tongue
down somebody's throat.
Know what is desired.

All the variations in sound
produced by the tip of my tongue—
no lip movement, no jaw movement,
no expulsion of air.

You're giving mouth-
to-mouth, from your lips.
Hardly decipherable yet
pleasing lyrics such as

apparently can be produced
stream out effortlessly even.
Impress upon the audience,
the best lips are now.

Your soft tab face is
swelling, sweet ololololo,
your soft tab face calling
for lips, tongue and throat.

Loose Lips

The networking of brain, tongue, lungs,
pharynx, lips, nose and sinuses gives
add-on features that help to figure
out the expected word sound
with good clarity. As I did,

you leaned in and pressed
your lips squarely against my
mouth, mimicking my every bite.
We simultaneously chewed.

Refer to my lips, and
involve the mouth, or tongue
in all your ulcerations,
the mucous casserole
of my oral cancre sores.

The throat refers to the tube
that starts behind this, also
the guy who played Marilyn
Monroe in a lip-sync performance

Big Muscles, Big Bodies, Big Trouble

I like my lips, and the lips
of anyone I've ever encountered.
The words—jaw, tongue and lips—
allow sound to flow.

Your vocal sound like uh,
not ah, the two sounds
stuck in your chest, kiss
progress on the lips.

Let me pull away to
see your lips sipping
wine in the distance,
and a growth of lips.

Your mouth, red cheeks, and
a swelling of the tongue.

Kiss and Tell

Kissing has become so common that many of us don't think there's more to it than just locking the lips. Smooching is not only a sign of love, occasionally there will be swelling of the tongue and voice box (the larynx), which may cause the throat to close and prevent normal breathing.

If his tongue is sitting out front shielding access to his lips, your tongue should do the same. If he continually forces his tongue down your throat, it's caused by the throat closing during sleep, cutting off the airway and waking up the body. If left untreated, it can increase the risk of "I Heart New York."

No Pain, No Gain

It was an oral solution of... it was of the chemical and tongue... it was for the form... and suckling as if to take it in. However, the patient difficulty of swallowing saliva, one hour after an oral comparison and patchy application of nutricosmetics or cosmeceuticals, left me impatient.

I grabbed my wallet and lip balm, and then, on impulse, grabbed my bottle of cologne, pulled out my waistband, sucked in my stomach, and gave myself an order to pronounce "th" as in "think" and "thanks." I will place the front part of my tongue against the lower edge of your upper lip and try to say 't.'

Oral Exams

Then you pressed my tongue down toward the floor of my mouth and had me say ah? like a patient. I figured you'd tell me not to stick out my tongue. Has this made it dangerous to be a student driver?

I went home later, laid around, played guitar, both of which came in noisy spurts like a horned-up Texan tongue flinging saliva at any be-boobed honey in sight.

A very thick shape often begins in the soft and moist skin that lines the inside of my mouth, nose, and throat. Can it also be found on the tongue and lips?

Fun Plan Foiled

In addition to having my own fundraiser, my plan was to bust loose from the Quincy courthouse by having my paramour slip me the tongue along with a key to these handcuffs. She lowered herself completely, slowly, and when her lips reached mine, her tongue invaded mine, twisting me around passionately. My con fell flat and now I'm in the Norfolk jailhouse.

"They got them a tongue-lashing, like in a rugby scrum," the judge said Sunday morning. "We spanked them a little bit verbally. They got put in the corner with the dunce hat on."

Tease Me Baby!

I was in my late 20s when I arrived, and I wasn't afraid to shoot from the lip, which, I'll admit, can be a little hard to take.

Now, my nose has begun to run, snot collecting on the upper lip. I don't mind, though, not tonight, not after my recent success.

A young father had his bottom lip and part of his tongue bitten off in a sickening city centre attack, then afterwards, he began to hum a tune.

It sounds like your sister's burning mouth syndrome. This 27-year-old condition causes a burning sensation or soreness on a person's tongue or lips.

This moisture on the lips would be comparable to placing one's lips or tongue on a flagpole, creating the opportunity for injury to the mouth and lips!

If you have muscle weakness of the mouth, jaw or lips, you can do activities that involve blowing and sucking to help you learn to retract your tongue.

However with the mini tongue you get the best of both worlds, all the lip locking action you could desire, coupled with intense 'lapping action.'

Finally I closed my eyes, laid the slice on my tongue and let it melt in my mouth. I could taste the acorns and grass the pig had fed on in its final months.

Untitled

Besides the lost teeth, all in the front of the mouth, I cut my tongue as well as the inside of the lips and gums. I required 25 to 30 stitches to close a cut in my tongue and an additional 50 or so to sew together wounds to the inside of the lip and gums. I sat out Saturday, needing 21 1/2 hours of surgery to treat four exposed sores in the mouth, some blisters and skin peeling; swelling of the face, eyes, lips, tongue and throat; I had trouble swallowing and breathing; and spoke with a hoarse voice.

A Glimpse into the Secret Insides

"I come from the bogeyman world,"
of rock and toil, "I don't
know, it's kinda fleshy,
in my mouth." A little startled,

I spit the beer
into my palm and
conscious to the stairs,
stood in the bathroom.

Then, weekend!
out with some
girlfriends we fired
the weekly lip.

Next, I was gloss,
counting participants
for news of private
percent lines and
patient contests.

Mucous comes in
the night, a gloss
on your lips, on
up to your skin.

V for Vixen

I only mumble through bruised lips with this badly cut tongue: "I didn't know anyone had this kind of power." I'll keep asking the good Lord to help me out, to finally settle the age-old 'spit or swallow' conundrum. I prefer the do-what-you-feel strategy.
Unless there's funky spunk involved, there's really no reason not to take a small sip for Flavour, drawing a little air in through your lips. I use my tongue to swill the wine around my mouth and chew at it.

My bottom lip seemed to be trembling as my teeth ground together and bit into a thick wad of chewing gum (or maybe that was my tongue).

Pepper and Salt

You placed one finger on my lips, to prevent me from saying any
thing stupid that might ruin the nascent harmony.

Presumably not to be dubbed,
simply to puck your lips,
and the pride of opening my mouth,
darting your tongue at Beauty-from-within

products are claiming to erase
wrinkles, give you shinier hair,
and will make your lips lock.

There was a door reading…

Our bodies don't need pepper
for survival, but we do need
to spice up our lives as surely
as we need to put rouge
on our lips and heels
on our shoes.

Sleep Surgery

I once dreaded the old saliva glands,
they tend to get in an uproar
when you shove your tongue
down my throat, eager,
a tongue lying for truth.

The wind is now blowing more powerfully, and it whispers loudly,
like a thousand lips shushing high up in the sky, as it sifts through
my mouth, as dry as the desert a second ago, now awash with saliva,
as this piece of cactus begins to take on the disturbing consistency
of raw flesh.

The back of the throat collapsing over the air.

It's bad for your teeth,
to brighten someone's day,
now, like a plague
that children find amusing.

Terms of Endearment

Nothing drives up my temperature.
Established lips for a moment,
coming from the right lips.
Are you running the tip of your tongue?

My heart is beating like the drummer of Deep Purple
on a good session.
I could not help squeezing my legs and letting go.
It is impossible to know anyone just by their words
and the movements of their lips and tongue.
A pure tongue not recommended for conversation.
There is a saying that the tongue has no bone.
That's the most severe concern.

Quick to Give a Glimpse

Slightly open your mouth
with a curled lip response
and inhale the smell of tongue
on the lips of those you know.

Aa? shall be ephemeral,
but many problems
originate in the upper
back part of the
salivary oral cavity.

Blood will rush to your lips, your body
will warm. Saliva will pour from your glands,
this is why kisses are wet,
your blood testosterone levels will surge,
and you will feel good.

The best ever lip,
mouth, or tongue, is
prepared for elimination, like
a kiss in training.

Doctors will open space
through an incision inside the lip
and dentists will look
for the usual lesions.

Oral inflammation of the mouth
ranging from redness to severe
inner cheek, tongue and lips can
cause practically painless
growths behind the tongue.

Attractive Attributes

First, to hold you,
the wine in your mouth,
purse your lips and
inhale gently as if

to create a noise
bubbling through children.
They find this immense
and amusing.

Use the upper back
part of the throat
to create an immense noise
that's indisputable.

As you hold the first letter 'a'
in your mouth, purse your lips and
pout. Lips send sexual signals,
inhale gently through them.

Try It, You'll Like It

Get the old saliva glands in an uproar.
Make yourself known,
buying stamps or filling your gas tank,
with shimmering lips.

Bubbling over an opened mouth,
an occasional "Honey" does nothing.
PS – I was swallowing my saliva,
tobacco spit increases the risk.

Pickles, liver, broccoli, asparagus, tomato juice, and
lots of other things
show the government is speaking with a forked tongue.

Another unlucky diner ate three bites,
he noticed tingling in his tongue and
the right side of his mouth followed by
a light feeling from a few years back.

Unspoken Fiction

Twiggy was a fixture around town,
with white face and two black eyes,
among the soft tissue of the poincianas.

Despite gallons of blood,
throat slicing galore and enough
smashed skulls to justify a certificate,
these horrors were not the scariest
elements of perfect texture—so smooth
they melt so delightfully in your mouth.

No tug of war among teeth, tongue
and throat for this exquisite rice cake!

Sharpening the tart edge of your tongue comes naturally.

Tasting spit salivating from your lips,
and a magnetic force to your grip.

A message of bitter hate
ignites like fire from
the lump in your throat,
sprinting over your willing tongue
before being captured
by pursed lips.

I have an oral thrush living inside my mouth

I have an oral thrush living inside my mouth. It's a small to medium-sized songbird with white patches on its breast, and to be perfectly candid, it's caused by a fungal infection of the lips, tongue, and gums. It is most common in the young, but I've never given lip service to being other than I am.

II. Sound Noise

Every week, I walk the sidewalk and that empty lot with my cart so carefully, that once you even stopped to say how amazed you were that you didn't care about the noise. You started to draw a crowd, and thanks be to heaven, there were two crying, in fact, tiny unmeasureable quantum fluctuations that would serve to nudge the ball off the top of the hill. That ball is horribly unstable perched up at the top of the hill. Correspondingly, this theory has an unstable vacuum. The ball will roll down the hill.

When you lived down that long driveway, I made sure your house number was easy to find from the street. I put up a stick with your address on it and fixed your mailbox. Privacy is nice, but having emergency services actually able to find your house makes you realize there's no true vacuum in which to work. It's possible to pare down your environment of distractions, and sometimes it's needed, but I've been able to create within a semi-private setting. Most of the time though, I'm in charge of distribution, and I have to say, I'm floored. I just can't keep up with the rush.

Mathew Timmons

I felt a rush of adrenaline, suddenly aware of what a terrible mistake it would be to get deleted without knowing this side of my ex-enemy. I ran a hand through my hair and looked back at you. Years of simply being with you, the greatest thing being that although life's fleeting moments pass by as fast as they come into our lives, we're able to say that we were happy even if only for a single moment. And you can continue to look forward to the next time when you come off a wave at high speed and you land and make a really, really loud sort of smacking noise and it doesn't sound healthy. We went out for the first time on a Sunday, and am I just being paranoid or can we just say that every event must be dragged down by some interminable logic, and that in fact the odd contradiction (generally through a remarkable individual) adds depth, just as the best characters have quirks and failures?

"I dunno," I said and bit down on another biscuit. While my childhood travails in the cleaning cupboard have left me with an obsession for vacuum cleaners, I also picked up a dependency on biscuits from many hours spent stuffed in the cupboard. I found a tube of caulk in the building, so I took it upon myself to sand down the primed wood and caulk it, and bought a can of Olympic Kitchen and Bath paint, which is truly waterproof once it dries and sets up. The vacuum brush grabbed a piece of thread and, well, I now have a white partition going down the center of my red carpet. Hmmm, do you think my mother knew about this? Thoroughly pissed, now that I messed up the carpet, I chucked the thought that it could ever be perfect again, so I tracked down a copy instead. Then, when I got the copy, I realized it didn't fit like the original.

After having made the decision to rush and then pledge, I became even more secure with organizations. Pledging was fun. There were no black sharpie markers, so no branding, WTF?, even so, it wasn't scary or intimidating when you cited a mix of all the factors pushing up oil prices including the weak dollar, a rush of speculation on commodities, and ongoing political concerns in the Middle East and in Nigeria. You found another flaw in the workplace just as it was getting better. I'm not too fussed although I can say that I wouldn't rush back for the Insect Vacuum treatment—It sucks big time … literally. I can give you a little security and I would also like to give you *Joyful Noise for three or more voices*, this month's free audio lesson guide.

I felt you picking up on my rage as we walked from the ridge down to the beach where the Gold Rush era SS Tennessee was wrecked in 1853. My first indication was a look from you—angry, hurt, reproachful, and questioning, all at once. I don't really know myself, I mean, I'm sure you can help me with that one, though I'd say if your rush fails, good luck! It's not a pleasant experience. I had been rather looking forward to some preventative maintenance. I used the shop-vac to suck out the drain line outside the house and also used the brush attachment to vacuum off the coils the best I could, and, to help some, I sprayed clorox in the drain pan.

The good thing about high frequency sounds is that it's hard to find where they're coming from. This circuit I've made can be mounted in a plastic box just like I have done. The noise it makes can be very annoying even though my name is well known in the audio industry as a maker of high quality sound and audio equipment. In order to make sure the audio from a movie can be interrupted seamlessly by more pleasant sounds like the "Warning Noise" or the classic "Ocean of Sound," something I've cited repeatedly is the method of noise canceling tests run according to the headphones placed over the ears model. The answer lies in various "helpful" things which get done to the sound once it leaves the ear. Also, I once read about a musical performance that, by accident of circumstance, became a process of slowly turning off all sources of noise.

Now, you may or may not be aware of Voice Command (and given the recent exodus, you most likely don't), but I'd like to announce the shut down of the "great emigration" based solely upon my faculty of volition. At last a bold, strong and loud voice of Orthodoxy will be heard to scare the croaking frogs from the stagnant disease bearing waters of the Ecumenical heresy! You will of course hear the voices of a few bishops, supporting this and other signs like: I cannot acknowledge my Savior on this campus which is against my right to free speech so I have elected to remain silent today in protest of my civil liberties being ignored. Many of the students here have said they'll just sway like a silent Tower of Babel, saying nothing and everything in a thousand different tongues. So moving, so filled with and emptied of suffering, so steeped in the music of a voice. Speechless before the truth, it grows softly under the veil of silence. These truths unknown. Spoken eloquently. Peacefully. This voice unheard. This voice unshared. The butterflies are here. They are fluttering… I can hear those silent thoughts again…

A witness to evil, a voice for the silent, and a timeless symbol of resolve now sings to us across the decades. The editors of TIME played your voice for me, singing an old song, adding annotations, photos, maps, and quotations. You sang without the instruments you loved, without anyone else's vocals to cover yours. They played your voice and you sounded so beautiful; everything that you were, captured and summed up. I cleared the supper dishes, wiped down the table, swept under the table, put away food, made lunches for those who took a lunch, dried and put away dishes, set the table for breakfast, and wiped down the dish drainer, counter tops, and stove. Close your eyes (oh yes, and sit down first), take in a couple of breaths and feel yourself start to slow down. Ask your intuition a question—it can be about where to move, what direction to take in your new life or whether you really, after more than four decades, have a truly independent voice?

Advocating for conservation, historic preservation, responsible growth and much more died on Saturday, leaving a silent void in the dark below. I squeezed my eyes shut; but your voice went on, every word seeming to drill into me. "We must leave the Apiary tonight, and go into the West," said the voice. "And if our hearts are true, the voice of silence ... the voice of silence will speak in stones." Love, Love is real, and there are no longer dreams. Love is a dream, and there is no longer reality. The law of non-contradiction is a contradiction. Is there a way of getting this silent voice to wake me up tomorrow morning?

When you got up and went to vacuum out your car, I didn't go help you because there were HORNETS in the garage and that is not cool. When your mom came over though, I helped her make dinner, and then your dad came over, too. It would be interesting to test out this practice in the face of the current recession, when high gas prices have quieted the streets by a decibel or two and reduced the number of restaurant-goers. Noise costs us in terms of health, but you were soooo into music, beyond what was typical of our peers. I guessed you were seeking sensory sound. Noise. We craved noise as we progressed through Occupational Therapy, until we became Sensory Defensive. You'd put your fingers in your ears. A silent protest! You said, "Yes, I'm protesting the political process in this country of ours and my voice shall only be heard in the pages of my journal! After Bush stole the election from Gore, I decided not to vote in an election until I could create a vacuum that sucks in people with principles who have a strong wish to help others."

Power trippers, those who use bluff, bluster, threats or power to get their own way at home and work, can sense fear or sorcery. My version of *The Good, the Bad, and the Ugly* is not very good. You and your compadres get into lots of drawn out duels before you finally get down to business. You seem to have the ability to move forward after your moment in the sun. Some though... like that guy who discovered the band Rush twenty-five years ago, he apparently decided that very day that he would play them so loud as to eventually cause a permanent loss of hearing. He is much too noisy and much too high, an exposition drawn out to about eighty-five sounds beyond the range of normal conversation. Measured for a level of moderate noise, a simple system can be an effective expander, where the threshold of sound is set by first analysing a section of noise. For this reason it's best not to clean up your originals. This is the shape of the impression of each repetition of the mantra syllable. These string together in my mind, as if there was a nickel 10 feet in diameter and one foot thick, bouncing and rolling down a straight path on a grey sphere.

Why am I silent on the issue of local authority? Do I have any grounds to criticize? Remember when we noticed that there were some civic organizations made for protest? I replied to all your questions, my friend. The first time you played my new instrument, you didn't want to leave it. I always wondered what it was that makes that noise, you said, let me take it home with me. To date the noise of my truck hadn't bothered you, but today it did. Again, you tried to high tail it out of here. Again I was able to change your mind and you came back. You sat in my lap right next to the truck while I massaged you and then I went inside to wash dishes for 10 minutes. You discovered that the vacuum cleaner was full and you left me inside while you ran outside to empty it. You came back inside to discover me sitting on the bench, tearing up teabags and sprinkling the contents everywhere. Go vacuum, then take a break and have a snack, maybe lie down for half an hour. I'll do some more dishes, take out the trash, dust and polish, get a drink... I feel more productive this way. So, the floors are vacuumed once again today and ready to be mopped once I get lunch done and we'll go outside for playtime then down for a nap. But, for the record, we're both pretty glad the vacuum beast is back in its cave for the moment. Sitting at our kitchen table about six years ago, we both asked each other, simultaneously, "What if we could split the wind blowing over a roof and create a vacuum to suck the roof down, instead of up?"

No, my opinion isn't any more valid than the beat reporter or columnist; I was a 25-year old liberal arts major whose only print journalism/sportswriting experience was a stint on the high school newspaper. That's not why I write what I write …and he heard a familiar female voice. "Is it Don?" Colby asked, on the bed behind him. Charlie shook his head. "Megan," he explained, but before he had the chance to actually talk to her, Colby grabbed his hand to take him back… On May the seventh, I will go to the studio and there will be scenes that no one has ever seen and we will shoot them that day and they will rush them to LA and they will cut them and those will be the final moments of the season. But this conversation leads me to consider a long term strategy. Our work should take serious consideration of thought and discussion within this arena. We can't rush the ending …the last thing you see—your lover, friend, soulmate—rushing forward, eyes going wide, as the blade slides into your body… You woke up screaming. Just listen to my voice, you'll be okay.

They say your abilities exceed those of all others, and even that no one had ever been as strong as you were, but they say you can barely stand the loneliness. Okay. So, you allowed my brother to lower your car about 1.5 inches, maybe 2—he was the only one, wasn't he?—and then the noise started. It sounds like metal on metal, a noise like powerful squeaking. Since none of us have ever heard anything like it, except from our forays into the realms of hard rock, I had no idea what we were listening to. When you drove up, I assumed it was one of those noise albums you've been listening to, like that EP, *Looped Power Lines*, but the failed brakes and removed steering column proved me wrong.

It's safe to assume that if you invest in one brand-new appliance for the move, make it the vacuum cleaner. Get one with a filter. If you can get one from a family member or at a yard sale that works, great, but this is probably the most important cleaning apparatus in EVERY society on earth. When Christian based morals are cast aside, crime and violence has ALWAYS filled the 'vacuum.' This is NOT UNREALISTIC FANTASY! I lived in that happy time without the choking influence of the state in every aspect of life. Personally, I have always felt my voice is better speaking than silent. The one time I did participate in the Day of Silence was my junior year in College. On that day my class "Gender, Sexuality, and the American Community" was not meeting. While the church has been mostly silent on the subject of sex, the world and the devil have attempted to make it their domain. The church has rightly proclaimed biblical prohibitions on the misuse of sex, but it has failed to speak out. When I say the mantra syllable inside my head, this is the voice that gives it a thought and sound. This mental track can also be silent, when I'm imagining a picture, scene, or shape I am doing so on the same level of my mind.

My, it felt like torture then, the sand and surf were yards away, and you were forced to withstand a full-body rub down at SPF 30. Decades later, you're still boasting milky soft skin while your friends OD on amphetamines. You must have seen some of the more outstanding flash at the bar, you may not think this complicated, and maybe even rough, but with good nutrition and a mellower sound, you'll soon be reading press releases about it all. The Occupational Safety and Health Administration once sent me a questionnaire asking: What was the first song you ever heard by Rush? 2112 from their album of the same name. It's a twenty minute epic and I love it. What is your favorite album of Iron Maiden? The Number of The Beast. Nothing else. My father was always anxious to get me used to working the soil, outdoors, where background noise was recorded and participants using their headphones turned the volume up high to drown out the surrounding noise. Finally, some of them, the young men and women, have learned to recognize the letters of the alphabet and read words by the syllable at short-lived schools set up to eradicate illiteracy. The effect of the silent version is greatly reduced. As students fail one by one, the County and the teachers remain silent. Public school transfer programs will obviously do nothing to help. Are we silent because we don't know who we are or what we are for? I wrote a chapter in a book called The Inside Verdict which I began with the words "This isn't working anymore." Well, is it any better now? Of course some of it is. But from you, who claim to be "the young vito/a voice of the people/mouthpiece for hustlers/a ventriloquist for doublers…" you seem to be quite silent.

Is it my place to decide what any artist should and should not be writing? I never really learned to do any of the fancy stuff but I love the rush of the achievement of becoming one with motion, the music, the crowd, it's all very addicting. I am really looking forward to how you look forward to seeing me, to feel the same rush of enthusiasm and eagerness that you arrive with and hopefully infect me with too. I see you there! It's a pity that this late rush will come in lists of nonsense syllables and the measurement of how long it takes to forget and then relearn them (here is an example of the type of list we'll use: bes dek fel gup huf jeik). With high-definition digital filters, our signal-to-noise ratios are getting remarkably better. It's odd, then, that we just keep getting noisier. Is there a connection between noise and class? Let's shoot a feature of you dancing in full regalia and reading from this book, Silent Voice of Creation. Let's go out and enjoy the sunshine!

When you're gone I have to get up and do your morning routine. Today that meant getting all of the children up, dressed and out the door. On top of that I have to do my morning routine. No big deal, I just drink more coffee. It's about time we decided to sit down and chat about this. My hope is that we can see there is more at stake here than profits, mob affiliations or additions to the house. We only have one world, and the long-term aim we've set down— to create an assembler, a microscopic device, a robot that could construct yet smaller devices from individual atoms and molecules. Even though, for the last two decades I have often cussed the fact that I live in a cultural wasteland and a vacuum of a small town, I find I'm actually more productive if I keep to myself and not concern myself with what everyone else is doing at the moment. There are so many names for what you encountered on your first day in London, "People soup," perhaps… You called to tell me you found yourself on the London underground at rush hour or after 10pm and it was human soup, a veritable hot pot of smells (some quite breathtaking), people and sounds. Last Sunday, at midnight, when you returned, I rushed out to see you and all you gave me was a sad look.

While it is certainly conceivable that creators might be willing to create in a vacuum, as discussed above, most want other people to experience their work. These other people are the content consumers and, like their fellow actors, I'm looking forward to the next training lesson. Level One: Wash any curtains/blinds/mats etc. that need doing. Level Two: Vacuum the floors; Clean the bath, toilets, shower and sinks; Wipe down the tiles and defragment the computer while doing so. Level Three: Declutter and dust the computer desk. Level Four: Get the car fixed. Whenever the engine is cold there's a sorta medium-high pitched sound if the clutch is pressed all the way down. The sound stops as soon as I release the clutch. My best description is that it sounds sorta like rubber rubbing, or like baby's bark, those kind of weird barks we've heard before. When I asked if you were alright, you took a breath that seemed to suck all the sound from the room. I felt like I was floating along, as if the world was fading out and you were the cause, the root. Then you looked up. Smiled. And the noise went on. You nodded once and turned your attention to the dialing device set in the console between us. You dialed the familiar symbols and we watched as outside the planet's dark night began to flash.

Mathew Timmons

First, you want to start with sweeping and vacuuming. Make a household chore list and use it. Learn to make awesome BBQ sauce and have some weekend guests over. Learn to make sprouted grain bread and to make cheese, or view some art and make a fursuit. Today is a good day to open yourself up, to allow yourself to wonder. But there's no need to rush. Give me one more week, and I can help you out. Can you wait to start until next Friday, or do you just, so badly, want to start today? Really, the crowd is just beginning to gather outside, and you can't wait to open? I think this launch could usher in a new, high-speed age of users in the U.S. Even if we do nothing more than pay lip service to the voice for now, it's time to stop the silent epidemic at the workplace. You are not alone! Many people are or have been bullied at work. You are not the first or the last person to fall prey to this unsocial behavior. But this knowledge isn't very comforting when you're surprised by a sudden noise from nearby, followed by a loud snarl and a few guttural growls. You go silent, listening, before a piercing animal howl rings loud and clear. You suck in a breath, mumbling something inaudible. Did you say, "Take me? Teach me? Lead me straight into another field?" Yes, you did. I can see more of the picture now, I look forward to hearing some normal head noise. If you go into a sound proof booth and normal outside noise is diminished, you can become aware of normal sounds. Because of outside noise, we are usually not aware of the normal sounds of the body.

I want to buy things when the price is low, but when does this occur? No one can tell exactly, but when a thing starts to appear as undervalued in its own index you can be fairly certain it's not going to stay down much longer. Using a clean white absorbent cloth, blot the area, pressing down firmly without rubbing for 30 seconds. Repeat this blotting process until the area is dry and odor free. Citrus based cleaning products may be used on almost any type of project. I can hear construction at the hospital (the hammering is very distinct), but not the high pitched noise of a bus pulling out. The car noises driving home are minimal, and the radio is just fuzz, sadly, but these are anticipated acoustic packages. The execution of the acoustic package is dependent on the noise limitations on site and the type of gas turbine used. Our experience enables us to determine and calculate the entire acoustic burden, including the sound. It's actually been said that in the old days, they used to do a very simple exercise called the Knee Clap—legs spread out, say a square wide, then bring the knees together. And, everything, every move, whether going forward or backward, has to cover this rush of new energy. You will find an enormous amount of life force energy available to anyone who wants to tap into and use it. Imagine the energy involved when flowers bloom, that life force energy is yours.

I couldn't help but try to rush through my presentation, a maneuver from your repertoire that I have incorporated in my attempt to steal the limelight, along with a cajoling banter, demeaning of both the representatives present, and condescending to the legendary Doctor in attendance. As an envoy over the years, you've helped me to become more and more like a voice of justice. I feel I can express nothing less than my true feelings. I try to take low emissions (near zero), excellent economy and other hybrid strengths from whoever has them. You moved forward with ongoing civic changes, before 23 million citizens, in their weakness, could stop you. But I couldn't hear you, the whole scene was too loud. Did you say, "I could kill them?" Speak slowly and loudly. Try the radio or the sound system features. I still can't understand you. Did you say, "I can't go another step?" I'm not looking forward to the ride either, I can assure you. As our fellow passengers finished boarding and stowing and belting up, we heard engine and road noise and saw the easy to see warning lights come on, and we awaited the revving of engines and the rush down the runway. Instead, we got the pilot announcing, "The computer read-out says, 'The rear windows do not open fully, but if you are what you say you are, this is going to be worth it.'" The pilot then added, "I imagine it won't be easy, but then the good things in life never are." You turned back, I leaned forward, and you clasped a hand on my shoulder, affection and warmth showing in your suddenly thick voice.

As I have reported previously, for as many as twelve days following your return, you could sit silent for hours, unresponding to touch or voice, or perhaps simply uncaring. Sleep researchers say most of us are either larks or owls, some of us to an extreme. The ideal day best fits someone like you, who rises at 6 or 7 am and hits the hay at 10 or 11 pm, so owls or larks should set their clocks back or forward a few. The strange thing is that, yes, the whole idea is that the only people in this game are other players, and that can create a vacuum. One of my big problems with sound is that very same fact. So, I integrated your clock's keypad-only mode with my phone's Matrix mode and threw the old Metal Tiger out the window. It's as if I just got a brand new voice, but there's this very high pitched sound, almost like hissing or a mosquito noise, coming out from the top of my forehead, right behind where my eyes sit. My experience with sound is that it works quickly and effectively without the hassle of a vacuum. I have never once confessed to integrating text and voice through the window of three dimensional voice visualizations or of including you in the conversation just to make quick, simple calls for easier navigation. I didn't say that. I did not say that. This is a classic illustration. You heard what you wanted to hear based on your own biases and prejudices. I simply recited some facts for you. These are not arguable. You can slip an old unmatched sock on your hand and dust as you go. For windows and mirrors? Use old newspapers to clean mirrors and windows. You'll have a great disposable cleaning refrigerator if you clean your refrigerator coils and drip pan. Vacuum the vents and coils to clean them. Dusty coils have to work harder to cool down the interior and contents of the refrigerator. Check the gaskets for proper air seals. "Where are they?" I asked. "They're right where I left 'em," you joked and were tugged forward a little as we did the rush forward and slow down thing, which generally meant a slower delivery into the forward line. Being a good sport, you slipped your arm loose and grabbed my hand as we set off at an easy jog towards the goal. Our rush was so good that the defensive side's pressure in the middle of the ground left the ball free. That which always gave the hawks a better chance of blocking up space around the goal was, instead, better still for us.

Apparently, what we thought was going to usher in a new age of data, turns out to be nothing more than a voice. We are not going to return to being the silent ones, we are not going to return to being the punching bags, and we sure are not going to return to tolerating ignorance, arrogance and constant insults. Again, I do apologize. This type of breathing activates the adrenal gland (your fight or flight mechanism) and your body is then constantly bombarded by adrenaline, noradrenaline and other hormones and enzymes used to get you out of danger. I know, a noise in the room left you unsettled. Considering our motors will be electric and used only to charge the batteries (hence we'll have less mechanical parts), our "engine noise" should be far less than most current vehicles, even most motorcycles. At first, I thought the noise was a voice and I mentioned it on the digital recorder for you specifically to listen to when you were analyzing the audio. Then there was another sound. The doctors said that the impact to your brain has caused you to lose your voice. Listening to your parents' comfort, but with nothing coming out from you, I broke down. During the stay in hospital, besides your still silent cries, there were just your tears.

At breakfast I got to meet everybody which was fun, fun… and then I rushed back to camp and got to volunteer for the day. I have currently been looking for Group Information and Special Group Greetings, some Good Classic Experience and a few notes in a hushed voice. Most of the time, when I team up with a couple medics, we're able to move our cart forward. The thing about the Gold Rush is that the entire opposing team will attack a single area. If we stop to camp, we won't move our heavy cart forward. And being on my feet is not a good idea for that long a time, but what I really regret today was my unexpected blurting out my opinion that, "For me, social movements start when individuals are free to think, create, ride trains, write stream-of-consciousness poetry, hang out in the garden for three years, or alternatively visit speakeasies in the middle of the night." You were down in the triple chamber structure all night, trying to separate heat and noise from the power supply, hard drives and mother board for cooler and quieter operation. Noise level is defined as Low (under 88 decibels), Medium (88 to 91 decibels), or High (92 decibels or more). A quiet high-efficiency 430 Watt power supply with universal input and active high voltage supplies many household items, like microwave ovens. The square waves from those signals inside the case cause lots of noise, and worse yet, many people either have non-compliant cases or just remove the case covers! A Boeing 727 co-pilot once collected 61 noise observations using a handheld sound meter and determined that there are three flight phases: Climb, Contact and Layout; Climb, Supply and Contact; and Climb, Contact, Release.

You may either sit or lie down, whichever is more comfortable for you. Cover your physical self with a light blanket if you chill easily. You want no distractions during your meditations so always make sure your physical vessel is hearing health. You'll have to rush like mad, hahahah. And there will be long queues outside the toilets. The water will be icy cold, but I guess that's refreshing. Then after bathing, we'll eat dinner. It has been raining lately, so there'll probably be lots of bugs inside the cage. You should be able to create a vacuum, if you can't the diaphragm might be punctured. I'll check to make sure the gap on all the spark plugs are the same and the correct size. Too small and you don't get a full burn, too large and the spark might want to track. You regularly rub your pet down with a diaper wipe which not only moisturizes the pet's skin but also gently removes loose hair and dander. A lint roller can collect loose hair, but will not moisturize the animal or make it smell better. I have always said that some tinnitus or head noise is normal. If you go into a sound proof booth and normal outside noise is diminished, you become aware of these normal sounds. We are usually not aware of these normal body sounds, because outside noise causes communication disorders and noise loss. Noise is sound that we have not selected to listen to.

Noise canceling is a quite an annoying option, but it's pretty much a high frequency that you can kind of hear when turned on without any music from head phones. It's almost the same sound as you hear when a TV is on, and this compared to what a single system achieves with outstanding detail and highly accurate color reproduction suitable for the demands of high-end video production—wide dynamic range, low color noise, high-contrast detail, etc. After a lot of work over the winter months, I got the bike back together, and it feels great, only now I hear a faint noise, kind of like a high pitch "whoooo" between 40mph where I can just hear it and 60ish where it's at its loudest. A Boeing 727 co-pilot once collected 61 noise observations using a handheld sound meter. He defined noise level as Low (under 88 decibels), Medium (88 to 91 decibels), or High (92 decibels or more). Also, the pilot determined that there are three flight phases: Climb, Add and Move; Seed, Leech and Sleep; and Describe, Present, Release. I rushed to applaud the recent Supreme Court ruling, telling our audience that it represented a huge, huge, huge move forward to undercut efforts to commit fraud this fall. Anti-fraud efforts this fall will supply our team with the evidence and stature it needs to rip apart the competition. Horton heard a who in the silent forest of information. Sometimes you just simply can't put an end to what other people are thinking and saying. I keep telling myself not to give a crap about what others might think or say. Heck, they don't even really know me yet, and I don't want to trouble myself.

If I cover the sensor hole in the left pillar, the overall sound is less, but the fan speeds up and is high pitched (like a vacuum cleaner when you cover the hose with your hand). I started a sound deadening project last week, and for this application I dissolved 3% sound in water at 95°C to hydrate it and then cool it down. Once the noise is cooled, you can brush it on one piece of the calcium infused fruit and lay another piece on top. Then we vacuum seal. The second most important part of the process is to stimulate business activity in order to increase sales tax revenues and to support real estate and increase property tax revenues. In the context of these realities, it is apparent that we are currently looking for a good, classic, hushed voice with experience releasing notes that supply more than simple information. You contacted a variety of groups, sites and specialty teams on our behalf, but in this society of researchers, no one can provide that kind of audio service. Layout, lyricism, nonsense, playfulness, stillness, description, intimacy, ambiguity—in a poem, anything can be an end.

You know how when you read a poem, you kind of hear it in a voice that's coming from the place where your ribs join? You were about to ask for your turn when a voice squeaked from behind us. This was a real voice, booming loud, sending molecules scattering every which way in giant waves through the air. "Do I ever get a turn?" "I think you should go back to Sleep." "I don't!" "Please. I was just joking." "Got you!" Then the room went Silent. "Yes?" "I miss you so much." "…" "I miss your smile, your eyes, your voice. I miss your everything." "…" "Say something!" "I'm in no rush to push my projects forward. Since I have a day job now it's not so important to rush and get to the point where these things are making money. I love my job and hope to be working there for quite a long time!"

Sometimes you didn't speak, and then people would scream and rush forward and I would duck under your glare and disapproval and wish to crawl up inside myself. But no one was ever as bright as you were; never. Say as I say, or you shall never go forward. I pray, since we have come so far, that be it moon, or sun, or what you please, and if you please to call it a rush or a candle, henceforth I vow it shall be so for me. The only exception comes when I wake up and seem to be perpetually chased by a monster to the extent that I suspect the monster has invaded Manhattan for the sole purpose of hunting me down. The silent voices of the people are begging to be heard and recognized; therefore we should stop and listen. You cannot know any nation, its past and its achievements, without first knowing the people who made all that possible. Last night a friend told me that his Russian friends say that if you rush to see all of Manhattan in the first few weeks, then you will have nothing left to look forward to. Maybe.

I glared at you for a while, giving you a chance to defend yourself. Finally, you sucked in an aggravated breath and shoved forward, your fists clenched tightly at your sides. "Nothing to say? Fine. Just, fine." This was the picture from the bridge. Let me lead the way. Begin with the head rests for the seats, and work your way down through all of the crevices to the carpet. Tip: If you have car odor you are trying to control, spread out baking soda throughout the car before starting to vacuum. As any sound engineer can tell you, noise can be most easily stopped at its source. Acoustical ceiling tile will keep the sound that originates in a basement recreation area from being carried throughout the house. Remember when Your Voice, My Silent Voice and Our Silence went to apply for the same job. Our Silence had more experience and education than Your Voice. During the job interview, Our Silence made a request for an interpreter and Your Voice opted not to. Two weeks later, Your Voice had a job and My Silent Voice requested the following information from human rights watch: the answer to the question was that only around 5% of people in each group chose "watchful waiting," or "active surveillance." A small percentage of people chose the job of sitting down with patience and explaining how these treatments would affect quality of life. Some tinnitus or head noise is normal. If one goes into a sound-proof booth and normal outside noise is diminished, one becomes aware of these normal sounds. We are usually not aware of these normal body sounds, because outside noise has a way of removing valuable high frequency spectrum from even the good parts. I have tried the high values, but that hacks the sound, creating even more noise. At low values it hacks the beginning and end of sound, but while noise cancellation does seem good, that's about all it has going for it because Your Voice still sounds muffled, soft and digital-like. Furthermore, my jawbone is too big and bulky to comfortably put into my pocket, but it does allow us to enjoy crystal clear conversations, free from annoying background noise.

Somewhere within the Wiemer Peto County area last week, I sent one semi out alone. I've had to send out trucks with double and triple orders from home. This is not too good, the expensive early game will eventually limit our rush, cutting down on the featured close-ups and shots of the actor's eyes dancing on the skates, skating backwards. When you worked as a scientist in Germany you made up spam and audio and TV and nanotechnology. And now, I've heard you're zeroing in on data for tinnitus and even Virgil and Eve and the Lady Neesa and more Unicorns and Lambs and WoW! When I looked up I could see you were the master of everything in the sky above and could see that you had taken your voice from the honourable Petruchio. Technology lets you sensor Technology Color using tips on audio removal for software recipes. Everyone, men and women alike, have a natural tendency to take the path of least resistance. My professor once pulled me aside and said, "You tell too many jokes." And later, my silent college roommate with phenomenal email skills told me over dinner, that I'd probably used up all my words for the day. For some reason, today, you stopped announcing things, and it worked fine before when you announced everything, but just now when you announced the beginning of this new movement you received a monstrous reprieve. I remained mostly silent. A new reform group of the Voice arose. Watch out my friend, take care of your voice. I'm in the middle of compiling New lyrics. I didn't realise there were SO MANY SONGS!! Oh my goodness. Even after we join forces our separate branches are still struggling to get enough members to hold quorum meetings and it is becoming ever harder to find people willing to put their names forward to be candidates. If we do nothing else between now and tomorrow night, let's at least get together and sing.

Martin Luther King Jr. said that "Our lives begin to end the day we become silent about things that matter." As loyal Canadians and Americans, we are compelled to work toward improving our communities, and that means refusing to be ourselves. Conceiving of one other than one's self at right angles of impetus and freeness, and self devoted caring, one is able to affect a rush of support. Hence, one's self becomes an oedipal prismoid, the Superego approves of the inner self in broad terms and with that comes a focus and depth granted by resolution. Tears jumped into the corners of your eyes at just that moment, but I could see you were fighting them away hard, so I didn't say anything. "Yes," you said, gratefully. "Yes, I would love to." "Great!" I said, a rush of relief and exhilaration pounding in my chest. Now we have special sensors to keep us from falling down the stairs. The system comes with invisible walls, which sends a signal to keep us from passing through the wall. And, we can be programmed to vacuum on a set schedule every week.

Yes, the whole idea is that the only people in the game are other players, but this can create a vacuum. Well, in my experience, one of my biggest problems is this very same fact. The stable auditory high turns into an auditory nightmare. I then develop a multitude of minor issues such as eye twitching, sensitivity to high frequency sounds, white noise, static, and distortion. I'm usually the last to admit my own failure, but will this note change with road conditions or be one continuous single pitched noise? What we have sounds like the old furniture noises but higher pitched. It's hard to describe but rather like a very high voiced version of our National Anthem sung by five children (ages 6-8). I don't think I've ever heard the National Anthem performed better than this! An entire arena remained completely silent throughout the entire performance.

I sigh at the thought of not seeing you again until Wednesday. Tuesday was your day for home visits, so there wasn't even the prospect of lunch to look forward to. We met last Wednesday evening outside that charming old pub, then returned to the job site and finished a long eight-hour rush to get done. I was sooooo tired. I hadn't worked like that in a long time. My feet hurt, my back hurt, I was mentally tired but LOVED IT. Just sitting with you at the Middlesbrough bus station wounded me. I tried to get a picture of the sign that said Middlesbrough but we stopped a little too far forward. I don't like Middlesbrough. Everyone has a place they don't like being and that's mine. You told me to go sit somewhere else with my mouth, and so with skill I rushed onto the court, dragging you and the bus driver away before you got hurt. My mouth sat on the sideline, continuing to film as you and I watched the fight, shocked by what we saw in front of us. Unfortunately, the microphone caught the sound of its own internal mechanism (I think it was the screen) and the video we produced had an annoying ringing noise.

Personal Wealth Advice, let's put a lens on exactly that, Personal Wealth Advice. I have two points I'd like to make. Whenever I saw you around during the day, you would say hi to me, and make sure I had gone to see which sororities and fraternities asked me back for the next night of Rush, and you generally helped me make the right decision to stick with Rush. Secondly, you taught me that sound is produced by a fan revolving at high speed. While for some it wouldn't be much of a bother, and some may even like the white noise produced, there would be individuals who hate listening to a constant voice. I fought to hold onto that lifeline, suddenly certain that voice was important beyond measure. It had been so long since I'd heard it. Other voices had come and gone, but never once had this voice spoken to me. Until now. In fact, you have been a voice for the silent majority on many occasions over the past eight years.

Your campaign has always been a tricky exercise, especially as you found yourself stuck with an unpopular president. I have to say it was refreshing to see police cars and not automatically worry about getting pulled over. Don't get me wrong, sometimes the evening rush hour traffic was a bitch. Remember when you and I were stuck between those two mountains and we saw a Flash on the horizon? You sat outside the mental hospital before driving home and woke me up to ask what time it was and if I was going to work. I told you I had to stop to get something and it just took awhile. Then I asked if something was wrong. You seemed upset. You could easily have picked up some noise-canceling headphones, which use internal microphones to generate another set of white noise sounds that drown out the ambient noise around you. You then reminded me that white noise isn't quite loud enough to cancel out our really noisy society.

Inside the dome of my mind's eye I can create a vacuum, with absolutely no atmosphere. Instead of repelling dangers, I simply form a dome around them. The requirements of this effort on my mind are disorientating, as I simultaneously performed the job of sitting down with our patients and explaining how these treatments were going to affect quality of life. Only around five percent of the patients in each group chose "watchful waiting," or "active surveillance," a small percentage advocated for scaling down workload. We were able to assist your valuable employees in scaling down work overloads by employing sufficient staff, improving systems and workflow, and by creating partnerships with other companies. You created a balance. You provided yourself with a good news team and affirmed that the exit interviews would not create any vacuum in leadership. Then, you rushed forward to take me into custody. When it was all over and done with, you escorted me outside and threw me in the back of your car, so you could drive me to mental health. The threat is now over, but my body has yet to recover.

As the angels reminded the apostles on that hill outside Jerusalem, the ending only comes when Jesus returns as judge to close the age, and exultation into glory; a victorious ascent plays an important role. The theory is most often attributed to a Scottish physicist who proposed about 40 years ago that the vacuum between the stars is not empty, but made of a fabric that extends infinitely in all directions. If anything, I toned this idea down to make it actually believable. Every opinion I wrote was based on fact and first hand observation. I guess the saying "the truth hurts" is spot on accurate, because I got many responses both for and against. I shrugged it all off, and a while later, crossed my arms again over my chest and the same thing happened, but even more pronounced. There was no pain just this weird "moving" vibrating sensation. It almost felt like liquid squishing around. It's certainly a possible trend, but it's doubtful that we'll move from "all free time being devoted to TV" to "all free time being devoted to creating." After all, one must consume things in order to create things created in a vacuum.

III. Basic Hearing

I.

According to Darwin's theory on how evolution occurs, a transformation is proceeded by millions of transitional shifts that form an unbroken chain.

This is unfortunately extremely difficult if not improbable to "explain," because remember, in the beginning the elite is the entire population.

While in real terms, on the other hand, a slight new low has formed that squarely puts U.S. authorities on the hot seat, under pressure to devalue their currency.

In reality, recipients live considerably below the poverty threshold despite increased program spending and the average monthly family benefit.

Whenever money gets low he drives to Mississippi to play blackjack, then comes home, and in themselves these actions are value-neutral.

She measures performance by number of concurrent packet users and idle time, or asks him for help (or she relies on the use of all three methods) while at the same time she will advise him to modify his demo and strike out.

He takes the time to add a new method and makes a further call for new parameters, checks for equal parity between basic variations and makes a request for a new speaker.

In step five he selects all the correlation coefficients having values greater than the detection level (the correlation coefficient is defined to be equal to one).

In June 2005, her response to his article somehow resulted in an apparent chain reaction that swept sequentially through the lower floors.

His original message showed up as, "I'll be hanging with ya'll every day! Ha! Ha!" and she responded, "You would be an excellent choice for a big up-tick in Quality!"

Running through the forest with a spear in hand and browsing online armed with a mouse is the best, because hunting and gathering are in our nature.

II.

Things are worse whenever he's in London, having the English comment about his Nigerian accent, in that it becomes more than simply an Anglo-America vs. Others affair.

She thought to herself, this is a fairly good representation of the concept we're shooting for, and she reproached herself that things would have been simpler if she'd had this in mind from the beginning instead of trying to wedge it in after the fact.

Though he is old with wandering through hollow lands and hilly lands, he will discover, rhymed out in love's despair, the flattery of beauty's ignorant ear.

An idea quickly formed in his mind and he set about with a new excitement in his legs when he felt the crotch rope increase the pressure on his midsection.

In her paleo-linguistic work and interpretation of the Göbekli Tepe, TYR became Tiras in the Bible, and Sseyr, the Middle Helladic form of Zeus.

He avoids dealing with the science wherever and whenever possible, saying only that carbon dioxide is the cause of climate change and that is simply not true.

She had no choice but to make a deal and give him back his "f-ing" money, and then she went back to work everyday from 9 to 5.

He contacted a friend, and has talked with him almost every day for the past year, in the sense that you mean it, as a matter of conscious choice.

She was trying to say that had FDR just sat on his hands and waited, there would never have been such a thing as American Empire in the sense of conquered nations.

When she comes to the door each night she can feel her little puppy pushing thoughts to her and as she opens the door she cocks an ear for a moment then responds with joy as she takes the puppy outside and lets her run.

Inside the receiving area he found new receipts on the pallets and began calmly counting them before responding to the job ad he had read while on break.

Hamas consistently refers to Israel itself as "the occupied territory," and when the Hamas terrorists are killed, they are counted by UN Sources.

As gender identity remains an unfamiliar concept for many, it's difficult to fully estimate the number of transgender adults today.

He never knew why people referred to the French as "Europe's Nazi whores," estimations by police prefects made in 1948 and 1952 counted as many as 6,000 sympathizers.

He clicked on the first line that was already invoiced in the previous step, step two, and then thought, "Is it possible I've made any modifications to the system?"

She referred to the ratio of 7 to 6 which defined a pure septimal minor third and of 8 to 7 indicating the major seconds or large tones between the two upper voices.

He remembered when Harry Belafonte made those comments about Powell, so much was contained in his tone of voice, and if it was supposed to be satirical, it was much less bothersome.

"Just don't do it" strikes a much better tone between partners, but somebody made the arbitrary decision to withhold this information from her.

He thought, "We should establish a cause and effect map of these somewhat arbitrary arts, and when they begin to gain consciousness, our map will become the new social tool."

She wrote: "You did not answer the question! What audio format did you use? Bit rate? Mp3 or wave file? Did you try using the wink on a pure tone, or Morse code?"

A wave of reports, official and unofficial, from American and foreign sources have included details of how plants and animals distribute themselves over space and over time.

She had experience in designing & configuring complex networks and hands on expertise in reviewing Technical Architecture to ensure all that was required.

III.

It was by means of verbal production that she concealed her personal intentions and shaped a shadow economy that ignored the principles of public good.

Perhaps a focused survey of areas where the mussels occur, near the estuary that he believes is in better shape, would yield their rough numbers?

Before she went to throw her stuff up on ebay she thought she'd let him know about the receiver packs (no ear buds included, except some crusty teenage buds).

She used concepts borrowed from the French sociologist Pierre Bourdieu, like "the shoulders of giants" that he wrote at the beginning of The New Atheists.

Strange things began to occur on Earth as a fleet of 50 huge, saucer-shaped motherships came to hover over major key cities across the world.

His initial folder was not set to MyVideos when it started an extender and as he arranged things in columns all they required was a simple left or right push.

The Strange Land is defined in the Oxford English Dictionary as "to understand intuitively," but her alternative course was called The Source Course.

He believed separation of mind and body to be a valid concept, but that it was very difficult to try and define a mental line.

She set out to find various files and compare numbers, to test more user threads and to define user multiplicity, to define "user" and the concept of user because it remained as yet undefined.

Natural selection, being conservative in nature, eliminates almost everything, and the micro-environment of, say, forest detritus, just doesn't change that.

She has experience handling complex support desk escalations; monitoring, troubleshooting, and maintaining complex network environments.

He created an environment to enable the generation of cubes via Analysis Services including the construction of Data Views and Fact & Dimension tables.

How could each and every successive beetle generation which speciated, ignore the environmental conditions especially in a world with designed roles in the food chain.

Through their state of understanding, Canadians achieved uniqueness in embracing diversity without conflict—What do Canadians have to gain from this?

She introduced a construct called "define" where users could save more complicated values, but on that subject, she wondered, "What are the valid values for priority?"

In the vicinity of the security fence in northern Gaza on Wednesday night, she asked her hundreds of followers if they knew who could help them.

He wrote an Introduction to Charles Darwin's *The Origin of Species* that emphasized two factors and inflated their apparent relevance far beyond their merits.

"Wrong choice of words," he admitted, but he honestly didn't think there was any choice when he walked into a party with that kind of everyday level of discourse.

She evaluated the results, at sea level, of a group of 10 high-altitude climbers with a battery of neuropsychological tests before and 75 days after the ascent.

Because the brain worked so well to record history for us, he guessed that people might tend to think of what might be happening in the world as far as social or political progress as related to progress occurring in the development of the brain.

She took the same approach with a stock; when she bought something for herself, she didn't second guess her choice; she selected her price and stuck to it.

She guessed that a device such as she described would make use of a switch and that the resulting homemade flashlight using LEDs would likely be smaller.

He made a list to describe what the software does, and what hardware and software is needed to use for any problems or troubles resulting from the use of the list.

She could hardly hear anything but revelry on Grafton Street; "Pardon me," she said, "Can the normal or choice word evolve in orbit around the source language?"

She had premonitions several times during the whole matter and she hardly volunteered herself for any further missions.

Nicotine causes a short-term increase in blood pressure, and heart rate, so he looked for a group of quit buddies and tried to join a group which had already formed.

A professional review panel specific to each theme was about to review proposals, so she sent a short description of her work and included various links to her materials.

The very definition of limited selection refers to i) a direct invitation ii) the shortlist of bidders (notice the plural usage meaning more than one).

She was responsible for handling the most complex quality assurance, conducted quality assurance reviews and developed and executed her own definition of quality.

The prosecutor claimed that the defendant referred his clients to lawyers and accountants who set up secret accounts, though ordinary clients may not have been aware of such secret accounts.

Different kinds of thought would form in his mind and he could not learn to differentiate or tell them apart and then he collapsed and the vet came out and cut his ear to let the blood out.

She was a leading figure in developing the next generation of computers reifying math, one of the greatest string theorists exploring all the dozens of mythical dimensions.

Her inability to string together a sentence that didn't refer to or attempt to account for the writing actually gave us something to discuss.

As the posting was already very long she moved quickly to describe her extension method and how the resulting string of digits could be converted to password characters.

In nature, sqrt (-1), has no preferred frame of reference as the old Newtonian inertial, but is coordinated with the imaginary magnitude proportional to it.

The power-sharing government was finally formed last week after months of fighting on the isthmus as Sri Lankan troops moved into action at Elephant Pass.

His mouth moved as he tried to express concern, but no real sound emerged as he fought displacement and dispossession in a relentless environment.

Her concerns regarding the OCA as being a viable partner in any movement included, but were not limited to, structures of accountability and the perception of the OCA.

What will the contractor do on this project, as it calls for a network and applications expert with required experience on complex routing schemes & techniques on LAN/WAN?

She tried the mod-11 multiplication process and found it quite a bit slower to do, and all the other 233,288 words produced unique passwords just as easily.

IV.

He noted that "massive accumulation" is a relative thing with regard to the pendulum cycle she described and that after shares go up a thousand fold, everybody's a billionaire until the pendulum swings back.

She scanned Sections 4-1410 and 4-1411 of the Zoning Ordinance relative to the NR zone signs, and realized acquisition of the Four Mile Run hinged upon a three-fold point.

The situation embodied a form of terrorism visited on the local populace very successfully by well financed and dedicated pressure groups.

She focused on complex and high-visibility content delivery in partnership with her clients to provide the most positive package including review, editing, creation and maintenance.

Spotting the zombie zoners in your past and your present will go a long ways towards changing your future, initially resulting in feelings that are so bad one concludes they must be true.

Roosevelt was, of course, quite aware of the intensity of popular feeling on the war in Europe and his consistently referencing "all the totalitarian nations" was intended to incite a war.

She felt that if she were allowed to use the original brand, she would gain instant approval for her proposal to establish The New Center for Good Governance.

She pointed out that common wisdom would seem to dictate that the U.S. support the Israeli Jewish population in their effort to gain recognition and acceptance, not to say security.

Her point made very apparent why corruption happens: "Clearly, they disadvantage smaller domestic firms and transfer money that could be put to better use."

A removal recommendation would be reviewed by a specially formed panel of seven judges who had initially voted to deny freedom to a man who under pressure had accepted a plea.

Concentration on pleasure and indulgence has caused a weakening in the kingdom of the heavens and of the earth that point to their Creator.

He expressed his fears that the poor economic situation in Palestine could lead to bulldozed homes and forced displacement on the settler-only roads.

Her figures showed that malaria was the first cause of mortality and morbidity in the city and the displacement of the population and the killings followed from that.

His results will help us to better understand how to implement climate change reform; a one or two decimal place change in atmospheric carbon could cause an apparent temperature change of 0.7 degrees.

She believed that a purposeful generation and definitely balanced creation could be the result created but the distance between these two things was not on account of space or dimensions.

What started as a singular strike against the structure of NYU's form, The Kimmel Center for University life is now officially a reclaimed space.

Marketing is a concept foreign to space advocates but the CMS portal is something that only requires an organizing team to lay it out.

It's the first time in a long time that we've had a political secretary of security at a time when Palestinian militants continue to strike.

In a bid to make a pre-emptive nuclear strike, the North's official media showed portraits of U.S. Secretary of State Hillary Clinton waving the U.S. flag.

He believed that modern capitalist societies have an apparent need for endless and imposed qualifying tests on voters, even if the results are pretty ugly.

The success of George "Washington" Bush was dependant upon his ability to clearly and publicly identify individuals who were intensely Evil.

She has a strong understanding of dense and sparse strategy dimension allocation report generation using Crystal Reports and Business Objects.

In mathematics it's called The Axiom of Choice; in biology it's thought of as how to banish the Black Magicians in everyday life; how to Cast out Demons; how to use the Trees.

The Technical Systems Analyst works with various functional areas to ensure their technology needs are met in a thorough and timely manner.

He often hosted the memory pathways through the nanites that acted in the scheme; to put it baldly, each creature who used magic was actually receiving energy from the Grid.

There are 805 railway stations in the whole country now, an increase of 318 from before 1988 when, at the time, the license fee was increased 166-fold.

She used the same HTML code he had defined in his page and then changed the output so all she had to do was change the script to debug the stage values.

The Harvard program, along with the community college efforts, represented a fitful creation of institutions and pathways for this new stage of engagement.

Braking systems have been created which can be taken one step further and because of this we are now able to build and take advantage of a new circuit.

Everyday webmail users, just like her, expected to be able to sort their e-mails by whatever alternative choice they desired until e-mail programs like gmail organized messages for them.

She thought that the announcement of the visioning process should be well publicized, so that they could hear from some of the people that Hazel had referred to.

He failed 2 out of 2 subtests in the use of uninitialized value and in pattern matching; at the time action was equal to definition and user threads were equal by definition, while user multiplicity was as yet equally undefined.

She had a set of twelve devices which needed to be charged every day so he could run communications, but he still didn't believe inconsiderate behaviour was a simple function of technological choice.

He said, "I just thought I'd finish these charts first, and sort of got sidetracked. ... I believe I hear with my little ear something beginning with the letter S." "Huh? S?"

V.

The ministry and his staff were not aware of this drilling; however, the activity resulted in small amounts of radioactive material being dumped in the waterway.

She assisted visitors with a legitimate need to gain entry to the facility and enjoyed her obligations to help with other incidents or conditions following procedures established for her post.

All the values in the set were blue and regardless of the different values a comparison of the different columns showed that any definition of the display would result in a display of definition.

He had to define an event in order to handle an event generated by button activation; this made it as easy for a python as for a programmer to figure out the oncoming of an event.

It's going to be difficult to advance the whole group forward without tackling any sort of practical considerations, although in the beginning we may want to re-visit some basic concepts.

During difficult times, he had to step up to the plate even as his office said the money, previously approved by lawmakers, was already being spent.

At the beginning of page 126 she discovered a question: Are there any situations in which you found it difficult at first, but then over the course of a few months everything changed?

The pitch of the vanes can be adjusted so that lift is generated during take-off by increasing their angle from a more horizontal setting.

His job description was to develop and maintain complex software specifications, translating business deals and to participate in pre- and post-implementation reviews.

Her job required at least five years experience in Software Quality Assurance as well as the ability and motivation to solve problems of moderate to complex scope.

"So nice to see you," he whispered softly in her ear, while he pulled steadily on her hair—each had their own thoughts and observations to relate.

She never actually arrived at the point where she had to "do the math," probably because in the past she did her best to undertake original research.

Whenever a sports fan gets mired in the past they become delusional or simpleminded and thus follows the goat talk.

Whenever a sports figure gets mired in the past it has fuck all to do with the modern period; they simply haven't got the skill to do it all anymore and thus follows the goat talk.

He never illustrates his points with bogus stories; it isn't necessary for him to lie; he has the ability to ask for and receive the past history of any object.

VI.
These bills are literally thousands of pages, pure and simple, very large, and worse they're filled with irrelevant questions and statements like: "The Canary Islands in the Pacific are named after what animal?"

His least favorite tone, without question, was from the same time frame she cited, which also contained his vote for the quintessence of pure dead jamming.

His statements led her to believe the damage had become apparent and the results of a microscopic examination of his brain confirmed the damage.

When the very terms we have used to describe the law become our reference points for the rule of law this means that the passage of laws will result in the rule of law.

Whether they are aware of each other or not is up to them; the location of the temple is hidden knowledge, and can only be referred to in cryptic terms.

The noise in the scan gives the roof more apparent detail; in addition, there is a max threshold unlike the others which are predetermined to show one result or another.

She was tasked with managing and resolving complex employee-relations issues and providing training in interviewing, hiring, terminations, performance review, sexual harassment, etc.

The national debt is just not that expensive in light of the dimensions of the current economic crisis—the torch has been passed to a new-born generation of Americans.

He pointed out that, in vitro, the bioactive peptide beta-casomorphin 7 (BCM-7) is yielded by the successive gastrointestinal proteolytic digestion of bovine beta-casein variants.

She announced she would be reaffirming her previously announced financial plan to integrate autonomous systems and add a number of complicated, time-intensive steps.

To establish a diagnosis of a compulsive disorder, and to find the causes of Cyclosporine toxicity, symptomatic behavior must occur; we must actually see the symptoms of Cyclosporine toxicity.

About this dimension of wholeness, almost nothing can be said, but she stuck to her opinion that in the Scheme of Things this is the largest generation in the World.

He revealed the true dimensions of the Eastern Partnership when he brought up the prospect of a new generation of Association Agreements.

He noticed that the left wanted to define what those on the right believed and were trying to express, while many of those on the left were afraid of the values expressed by those on the right.

She wasn't sure why, but some people complained about the negative comments previously posted in the newsletter regarding Chili and many said that walking up or down steps hurt their knees.

The seventh partial is mighty low compared with a minor seventh; in a harmonic series all values are defined by whole-number ratios.

Many of her model fitting skills did not fit the original description, but actuaries have a long history of valuing complex non-traded liabilities.

Although this concept is known all over the world, many countries have seen their rates increase since the beginning of the new millennium.

Modern forms of public choice theories take into account real human experience so as to include more of our infinite nature into everyday living.

His ministry may be unwittingly contributing to the perception that governmental programs are cultivating our love of mercy while choking out our ability to act justly.

Communication truncates thought because the details of our subjectivity are like the gentle ears of a child and these are acts belonging to creation: thoughts.

His signal was decoded and quickly completed; it can now be accessed using the VK standard 123Hz sub tone with GD0TEP's moon at six degrees.

Along with many others, she had previously attempted to submit similar applications to set a plan for researching and implementing further steps in judicial reform.

If she sets a count in the page then whenever it reaches the page again it counts input type as hidden when it submits the count and in this way it doesn't change the value of the form.

"Thanks again," she said, "for all the excellent answers and help so far and let me know if any other thoughts come up, but if there's nothing else, thanks for the ear guys."

The function of the vector state index when referenced against the value of the defined state as lambda might help when comparing the big picture to code logic.

While it is sometimes helpful to review the Federal guidance, they must be read closely with a realistic description of your project in mind at all times.

He said, "I don't have any children of my own here to help me, you know you boys are like sons to me." "Yes, ma'am." Well, a son should not be having thoughts like that.

She found a facsimile of the Geneva Bible and thought it quite difficult to follow; for example: "In the beginning God created heaven and the earth."

He found allies in the anti-communist cause and made friends in various small foundations, small groups and viral organizations that attempted to threaten established media institutions.

Since they were just at the beginning, and their mailing list really was in the service of defining Craftsmanship, she wanted to note that she found Point 5 to be a bit difficult.

Having surmised he'd be a sympathetic ear, she thought he had volunteered to listen, but racism is still so strongly clung to in the Old South because the inequalities persist.

The result of ignoring a pathetic fool is that it's just more and more and more easy to isolate a fool into a small number of specific, easily identifiable threads—all relating back to the pathetic fool.

Having surmised he'd be a sympathetic ear, she volunteered that old saying that says just about everything concerning class.

His illustrations showed ordinary bamboo sticks with 2 horizontal lines and he intended to cultivate an element of suspense in the text which he hoped would be generated by the notes in the footnotes.

She claimed that flocking is horizontal and occurs at irregular intervals, forming clusters while tumbling is vertical, a relationship between two or more strands.

VII.

His protest was uncalled for, nor was she prepared to tone down her righteous invective against such inanity unless he finally gave in to changing his long established pattern of pure, unmitigated evil.

For the type of pure amp tone she was going after, she noticed a huge difference in comparing her own amp to a good Twin or Super Reverb.

He referred to "the coachman" as the source of information and spoke of one Union general who wrote that he counted on black spies in Tennessee for information.

Establishing true friends, mentalities and positions along with cultivating a prayer life is definitely key; doing without such things can be the source of much gain to the enemy.

Finally, she was able to inspect the resulting parse trees (in this case their clarity is all pretty so-so) and she moved on to develop a feature-based grammar that would correctly describe the following lack of clarity.

"Hi again," he wrote. "Perhaps I did not describe my question clearly: Have you used this starter before? I wanted to ask about the taste of the resulting bread."

She could also define variables that store the values of these pointer types, which if converted to common types and compared, would compare equally.

What he had in mind was something akin to *cf.*, but it would not compare values, only the names of variables; it would not care whether the two data points were of different values.

Human faculties of conception, perception and learning caused him to question the attributes of god; he asked, "If your god so clearly exists why are there 57 varieties of his Heinzness?"

She found little information presented in the background research that supported his scheme and issued clear supplementary guidance for the current rule.

He made sure that he himself was not around to cause any inconvenience, but he was firmly opposed to the proposal called for nor was he prepared to tone down his righteous invective against it.

She wanted to take a step back for perspective, but not only that, she also wanted to look around at the industrialised food system.

Is wilderness (or nature) only valuable to the extent that people "use" it? If a tree falls in a forest and no human is around, does it make a sound?

A particular style and norm of word choice evolve in orbit around the source language that surrounds a person every day, unless you go to an Esperanto event.

It seemed to her that the 2:1 step up ratio of the matching transformer might easily affect the dead and allow for the small corrections discussed previously.

She has an ear infection and no one from his family is willing to put up the money; she's too good-natured, but he always thought she played the dominatrix.

The Kinglake area was a nature-loving community of tree-changers, although it didn't quite have Victoria's perfect storm of winds and forest types.

The result, amongst a group of similar atoms or molecules, is that the electric dipoles create a distortion effect in the far smaller constituents of each atom.

The report quotes the established principles of an effective drug program and that there is little cause for building in penalties, because the incidents are negligible.

Although Planck insisted that radiation was simply an aspect of "physical reality," it would come as a surprise to Lee Smolin and a generation of physicists who have been working on a theory of quantum gravity their whole careers.

He badly needed the international community to provide focused support, in the form of both incentives and pressure, to send a clear and consistent message.

She was responsible for the development of testing and implementation processes for complex systems and assisted technical management in the description of position.

Differences in rolling resistance are apparent when one rides over smoother terrain and when similar negligibles were added together she was able to get a significant result.

In fact, the only visible cause that produced maggots large enough to decompose the man's body so quickly came from the side of his body laying on a pile of compost.

In reviewing the job requirements, he didn't know if he was interested in helping customers to understand and manipulate large amounts of complex information.

The only failure she saw in the small and large units was a drastically reduced battery capacity that she suspected was due to electrolyte drying.

April 1997 introduced the modern 'Paris mulligan' rule; previously, at the end of a turn or step, the mulligan could be taken as many times as desired, then the distinction of the mulligan wear-off was introduced in order to eventually lead to the end of a turn.

The structure she discovered had formed spontaneously and unexpectedly when silver nanowires crossed to create fresh content and she believed it could reduce another heart disease risk factor, high blood pressure.

He produced no reduction in any of the parameters considered, but his results gave further support to the hypothesis that gags actively participate in the process of silencing.

Differential group tendencies not withstanding, a majority group simply has more members making it more difficult to ascribe bias-motivation whenever there is doubt.

You'll remember when home mortgages were seen to be essentially guaranteed by the government, and that, as a result, it became apparent the homeowner couldn't win while the banks certainly could.

Ironically, they can slow things down because they simply use way too many variables, even though both primary figures are below the value of Physical Memory (K) Total.

The probability of spontaneous generation is about the same as zero; however, the macromolecule-to-cell transition is a jump of fantastic dimensions.

A better future for the next generation was never a priority before; therefore, a macro policy integrating social dimensions is now necessary.

Although he never thought of it as cruel when people did it to their pups—and a six-month-old dobie pup with cropped ears brings in a much bigger price—he didn't like the practice.

Like a single tree falling silently in the forest, he admitted there was no describing the content of one's mind and the nature of one's relationships with others.

Why do you insist on appealing to Scripture, when it is so apparent that you don't believe it? You worship man's view of origins.

From near black to pure white, she saw 5 to 7 stops of meter change and wondered if it was possible to get the snow in the right tone.

He noted that the meaning of "protein group" had changed and that any network of proteins with shared peptides were now to be counted as a "group."

The United States' use of taxpayers' money to fund clearly partisan misadventures distinctly skews the perception of Cuba's current geopolitical realities.

In the event that he truly believed it had to be a choice between him and McCain, it would be much easier to observe in everyday life these kind of purely antagonistic relations.

"But hey, it's your bachelor party," he trashily repeated in his friend's ear as he shook uncontrollably at the mere thought of strippers, but an hour plus later, there they were.

VIII.

We learn much more from forward looking models and the same arguments hold for P-values, but they shouldn't be used to compare three (or more) models.

If a spammer refers to the home page as the canonical version for thousands of pages, would it be counted toward pagerank?

We can discuss the question of what causes the outward radial as if it only needs sufficient force to establish the imbalance at one point.

The questions and previous analysis we have offered will have to be answered with time as this will undisputedly be a step backwards for democracy.

Team Obama is taking a giant step toward nationalizing the mortgage market as nationwide about 4.2 million previously occupied homes were listed for sale.

National security policies toward enemies beyond the state have changed relatively recently especially regarding people who have had little or no experience with firearms.

It's nice to think people will step forward and slog through previously proprietary language on any operating system to drive the interface.

A further battle was fought by the Eighth and newly-formed Tenth Armies in Tirpitz under strong pressure after Hindenburg had initially demurred.

"On further thought," she said, "I'm not going to add a 'claim your bug' step just yet, I mean, say we have an internal user that has previously filed 6,000,000 bugs,"

He flagged for further examination, "use threads equals define, use multiplicity equals define, use perlio equals define," while his real problem continued: "use d_sfio equals undefined. Bailout called. Further testing stopped: Can't load module FAILED-----"

This is just the basic in your face kinda stuff—there is more crap that goes on in the classroom every day than we expect our teachers and admin to acknowledge.

Shows how little you actually value AA and it shows how little you respect the members of your group; simply calling someone an asshole and pointing that out whenever it's obvious doesn't really help.

One thing he got a lot of positive feedback on was the fact that MB is simple and doesn't have a backend to configure etc. and that for most users it's simply a case of logging in.

IX.
His position would be filled at a higher grade upon review of skills and qualifications, but his typical daily responsibilities were primarily to attend technical reviews.

They are clearly moving ahead with the next evolutionary steps undisturbed by UN sanctions or technical injunctions, but genes are limited, with about 30,000 total, and natural selection would take a while to work itself out.

I think the word and the concept of "cartel" fits quite well, if qualified in the manner that it was; it's often very difficult to get inside other people's minds and tell them what to say

The fact of the matter is that Political Correctness has a history, a history that is much longer than many people are aware of.

He still worked at the main office and thought he'd have a little fun with ear worms so he decided to open a thread dedicated to that exact topic.

She created and maintained page meta tags (title, key words, descriptions), demonstrated an ability to capture complex ideas and expressed them in a clear manner.

He had simply forgotten the occasion, but he was aware of the fact that at the main event, the folk were originally referred to as a "host of warriors."

The arrogance the Holy Spirit teaches in these thoughts from God made her wonder: Did these same proteins just decide to construct an ear when there was no ear?

It is difficult to define the concept of propaganda thoroughly and precisely; for example, the stories spread throughout the world at the beginning of the war about German soldiers chopping off children's hands, were simply untrue.

Eight years later, Obama walked into the Oval Office to find almost $11 billion dedicated to The Wigan Pier Quarter Interpretation Project.

Because the mind is, the organs function; and if the mind doesn't, there is no ascribing God-hood to all your internal and external objectives.

If the dump doesn't show a column called Page Include, or if that value doesn't look like a decent template name, then the query, or something else, is the problem.

After he deleted a number of entries they were still counted in the numbers of texts in the archives and the code bX-9u1kis appeared when he tried to fix the problem.

First, she established that any clause in PTW is problematic in a way that can be fixed, and she didn't see why it caused any sort of double standard.

She participates in design review meetings with Division and Area Project Managers, and provides problem-solving support on the more complex system failures.

He pointed out that, "Many newspapers have English owners/ editors/ columnists, as I'm sure you are aware of, in England," a country he so bluntly but aptly referred to as "that shitty little country."

Simply leaving off the extra two columns, she added the requisite foreign key and joined the table to itself whenever she needed either or both of these values.

It is apparent that she was not at all concerned, so he stuck to shredding her lame mission statement as a number of his colleagues had been murdered as a result of her negligence.

Her point to the moderators was simply that these are difficult matters and she was not one of those scientists who dream of mass slaughters of bureaucrats in an allegedly cold, value-free world.

He was missing something simple but what—pow! 'Decimal' and 'None'—whenever he tried to save the foreign key model he thought the problem might be in the related model type.

Then it started to rain, and didn't stop the rest of the day; she was on private property, and she had to secure prior permission to use it.

She stayed out the week previous and missed (well she wouldn't say she missed much) hearing the view that the nation's private financial system should be maintained.

X.

There's widespread perception and concern that we are losing something that has existed for generations while training in most skills has generally been limited to basic concepts.

You might also be interested in "what are the differences between Borland/Delphi/Kylix languages." Don't just post your assignment! Be aware of limits.

To avoid conflict, she thought it should be noted there existed the perception of the elite never recognizing that training in most skills was generally limited to basic concepts.

Still, he wanted to say that enabling was the better description of their relation, but his view was not supported by a review of empirical information.

It is difficult to say definitively what Tantra is or is not before we can finally explore Sarkar's concept of Tantra as a tool for social liberation.

If you access the array with a simple console log with multiplied weight—something like this: type equals "hidden," name equals "weight," value equals "value"—then the script works properly.

AppModule Name now only contains the AppModule name, not the class name, which is a problem but can be solved just by using the original code whenever returning an NVDAObject.

The tutorial shows how to create a simple wiki with Turbo Gears 2, but it requires the creation of a new template named 'page.html.'

A six-month course is a wonderful choice for a basis in history and theory, and you can simply attend classes as an "overnighter" from 8:30pm-4:30am every day.

She presented a full review, with a detailed description of the rules system used, and a complex combat system, but it lacked the editor and multiplayer gameplay.

Even if a Palestinian state were established on the principles of secular democracy, and even if full equality were possible, wouldn't the basis of that secular democracy remain predicated upon our appetite for oil?

He counted the nominations at the end without having to refer back to the first post, which was wonderful, but must have also included the vote.

He was sloppy about return values, but now he's fixed that as well, unless your system requires all attributes to be defined.

The reason that she turned away from religion or god towards fatalism (which includes the concept of good or bad luck) is that fatalism doesn't require a belief in gods.

She designs and reviews quotes of complex network solutions and services while citing specific analysis on technical requirements specific to customer needs.

The United States & Europe require 500 million tonnes of corn and cereals for the creation of bio fuel, while in Cambodia the military junta has taken the concept of bio fuel to heart.

He had a choice that needed to be made every day of his life; he could either work his guts out to afford one of those things, or not.

This is rather free of context, but he thought its tone might spark her curiosity: "Progress is made when you explode someone else's pet theory."

Over the years she gradually made the villagers realise that their survival is linked with nature, and now, no tree is felled in Baripada's 1100 acres of forest land.

He said, "Looks like we made it! Wild Thing Tarzan Boy! Now we're Free Fallin'!"

XI.
While all reasonable steps have been taken to ensure accuracy, the torque at 1500 rpm is now more than the previous max torque at 3000 rpm.

In Duleeps he is still the incumbent as he eats 10 plates of idli sambar everyday. "Good!" she said, "Glad to hear his criterion for selection is so high."

Each heart won over is a victory! The day will come when several dozen start singing the "Internationale" and we have no choice but to overpower the rest.

In the meantime, I don't suppose you have it in you to give an old woman a ride?—He grinned from ear to ear—Sure, Baby.

In practice, whenever she gets a record from the database where a field simply represents a Null value, she makes a note, knowing it is another matter entirely.

Accountability to a politician is what a heart attack means to your brain unless you've spent one million dollars per day, each and every day since Jesus was born.

Choosing to go after the Khmer Rouge leaders, whose legal guilt is far more difficult to prove, is pointless—in economics, this could easily be demonstrated with the concept of means-ends matching.

Her analysis of these 250,000 tree records reveals that, on average, tropical forest trees are absorbing about 18 percent of the CO_2 added to the atmosphere.

Most international criticism directed at humanitarian issues referred to this kind of humanitarian center and reflected a shared interest in understanding.

At Birkenau, such an operation was usually performed by means of Zyclon B and it was common at the concentration camps for many of the prisoners counted there.

His final analysis of 250,000 tree records was published in Nature: "Tropical forest trees are absorbing about 18 percent of the CO_2 added to the atmosphere."

The difference (the square root) is very small so it is difficult to measure; in fact, the symmetry is only apparent and results in the slightest difference of calculation.

If your needs and goals are simple and you're interested in only a small number of groups, you should make reference to your preferences when signing up at Ye Olde Inn.

XII.

It was time for him to step up and actually do something in and for the community instead of continuing in very much the same vein as those that came to the forum previously.

She wondered how her character would be formed—Would she have this? Would she have that?—it had something to do with the pressure of being a double agent.

He can create a custom skin and apply it to his project at time of generation, but he's still not sure how to find out the dimensions he should use for the contents.

Whenever practical values form a practical point of view, objects become much more important because those are the things that really carry the state.

She was one of the generation of poets who must have been blown away by the elaborate transformation of an immaculate modernist home into a dilapidated 1970s drug den.

Whenever he accesses an Array he has to take care that it's already filled with the right values and the easiest way is to do everything in his power to self-populate that Array.

True to style, Einstein swept away the concept of "ether," but Einstein's work stands out not because it was difficult but because nobody at the time understood it.

Fatalism, which includes the concept of luck (good or bad) of secular societies, is beginning the process of de-integrating religion and superstition.

Her description of the bubble and bust in her report showed a very good way of valuing complex non-traded liabilities while maintaining professional standards.

XIII.
In her program, such pointers would be defined as the structures used to hold the pointer to the "value" portion of any association.

With the Word as His counsel and Spirit as His tool, He formed heaven and said there was nothing he could do to relieve himself of such pressure.

She saw a native tea tree plump with flammable resin and thought it should be included along with other forces of nature in any model.

He had a sensible approach to nature vs. miracles and believed that when a tree falls in the forest and there is no one there to hear it, it makes no sound.

Someone should have thought about the future when they sent a rocket scientist to predict that it will take a prohibitively high level of funding to make an artificial ear for us.

A Doji is formed when the open and the closed are the same or very close; the body, then, represents an overwhelming buying pressure dissipating the selling pressure.

As she saw it, whenever his mailbox sent out an auto-reply, that auto-reply cascaded throughout the company so she decided each user would simply have to do without auto-reply after that.

His uncannily precise description of the crisis pioneered the mathematical analysis of chaos and complex systems.

His position as Business Analyst allows him to take a leading role in designing systems and programs to meet highly complex business needs.

Russia's head of state now acknowledges the seriousness of claiming economic difficulties for the purposes of trying to establish any legitimacy for anti-semitism during years that pogroms occurred.

She interfaces with existing external consultants to assess the current business needs and reviews manpower needs so that they are in alignment.

He stood sufficiently distant from the video screen so that he really needed his glasses to see it clearly, leading to his perception that there was not much of a market.

She was forced to tone down her claim when it became apparent that a lack of paradox was partly the result of the diffuse, but ever-present paradox.

Honestly, he was hearing things if he thought he was getting a better tone; she runs a 25w bass amp and gets all the clean signals she needs, right up to the edge.

Apart from these two particular issues, a snapshot of raw time drift usually makes the drive faster, but with the windows on the right and the added "serial" parameter, success tends to flag.

She was getting a little bit of support for her apparent evil and "urbanistic" styling choices, and she urged her critics to wait until she was done, but then she heard the call of the track!

She wanted to be clear about her intentions; we must know what we want, as success is decided only by one's ability to become integrated into the environment.

At the beginning of the semester he went over his syllabus thoroughly because he knew more than anyone how difficult the issues might become.

XIV.
If somehow she had been empowered previously by being rude, she now wanted to talk about engineering working social systems for the discussion group.

Investors were clearly concerned as SunTrust shares took an 18% beating, but this only reflects the least of the market's perception after looking at the ratio of share price to book value.

It has been clearly demonstrated that an ape has the same fundamental power of perception as any human being, though not as much perception power as a human.

He found three downloadable isoline worksheets listed under "Humor and the Dimensions of the Geritol Generation."

He lost weight while breast-feeding and milk production were being established and exhibited less motor activity but more eye contact and his normal behavior state was crying.

She was aware that withholding your breath and slowing your heartbeat causes a failure to thrive, which is most often discovered among infants.

He was getting a little bit of support for his apparent evil and "urbanistic" styling choices, and he urged his critics to wait until he was done, but then he heard the call of the track!

She was reassured to hear stations from all over the state and interstate on the Net, demonstrating that we could, if necessary, establish communications.

Other than to re-iterate the concerns raised above, he was interested in the nine hundred and thirty nine cases of elder abuse referred to in *Age Concern: Elder Abuse and Neglect*.

Jesus even referred to the Father as "my God" (John 20:17; Matthew 27:46) and similarly, the apostle Paul referred to the Father as "the God and Father."

He was injured by an insect and the burns on his back were treated similar to a sunburn; he was, however, not aware of the team within the cavern.

XV.

Along with a demonstrated talent for analyzing and streamlining complex work she attended and participated in design review sessions and consistently provided the best approach to a problem.

He found it difficult to re-establish the rule of law in a split cabinet, and of particular profligacy were the ministers of state, positions created for show more than anything else.

During adolescence, defiant underachievers begin to see that identity itself is often viewed as an abstract concept, making the task of identification rather fluid.

We have no divorce or family planning, so the net result is that men cannot afford to discount God's providence in this world most of the time.

She said, to sum up, that using distinct keys for encryption and signature was the first step and losing your signature key did not invalidate previously emitted data streams.

What you "see" as a star, is actually the result of a quantum interaction between the local field and the retina of your eye.

She liked trying to educate the American people about dimensions, and, she knew, there was actually a risk of having the first generation of living Americans.

After a lot of pressure there was a duct done for only half the required area and before he closed for the week he made sure the by-laws were discussed and formed and that he was ready to get registered.

In order to distinguish himself from the others, he referred to himself as Damian, and like Saint Peter, he counted earthly gain as nothing, and heavenly gain as everything.

XVI:
Her community does not push image generation machines; on the other hand, her community has pointed out the interesting property that for N spatial dimensions there are $3 sup N$ dimensionalities.

Please send descriptions of care support coaching for patients with chronic and complex conditions by fax or email only using Requisition Number 7993.

XVII:
So there it was and almost everyone thought The Secret Scripture was very strong, but she confessed that as a 21-year-old undergraduate she cocked a sheepish ear.

"We can recreate dimensions of time in the gospel," she claimed, a Professor of Religion at Princeton University. "The gospel of Mark was written at least a generation before Matthew."

Let us see how Singular's hilb command works: first, sage prints a singular eval type of sage4 that has definition but no value, then it compares sage, which has value but no definition, to sage4.

A sphere in synergetics has a radial value of 1; the surface area of the sphere is defined as four times pi times radius squared (to the second power).

A mistake is committed whenever it is argued that a proposition is true simply on face value instead of reading and understanding its possible fallacies.

The Lightsmith building is available whenever he needs it, but it does not sound like attending would do him much good, to just sit, listen and write.

XVIII:

She usually had a choice of sending a saved message, an envelope icon or an email and this choice was visible to her when she opened the message box.

XXI:

He was not sure if they took skin form behind the ear or not, but tried to stay positive and live for the day.

...

Well, as they say, you can wade through a 42-page chapter of the fine Manual that refers to the previous topic (yes, I counted the pages); or you can do the following...

A Note On Process

I. Lip Service

The first section, *Lip Service*, was composed using Google news alerts, employing four search strings of four words each over the course of one month from January 1 to February 1, 2008. The resulting text was then lightly edited to highlight its lyrical qualities. All material was kept in the order it originally appeared.

Lip Service search strings:
lip lips mouth tongue
lips mouth tongue throat
lips mouth tongue saliva
lips mouth tongue spit

II. Sound Noise

The second section, *Sound Noise*, was composed using Google blog alerts employing sixteen search strings of four words each over the course of one week from Monday, April 28 to Monday, May 5, 2008. The search terms were pulled from a Wikipedia article on the mechanics of speech production. The resulting source text was then lightly edited with all material kept in the order it originally appeared. All pronouns in the text were changed to gender neutral first and second person pronouns and verb tenses were shifted. Once the forty discrete pieces were composed from the source text, the order of those forty pieces was shuffled according to the author's prerogative.

Sound Noise search strings:
manner speech sound nasal
contact production place stop
vocal air articulate vibration
flow oral voice voiceless

voiced voicing silent release
burst resonant resonance cavity
sounds noisy noise high
pitched pitch represent momentary

pronounce vibrate brief call
called syllable increase together
behavior liquid substance dialect
resonant outward power lungs

ribs diaphragm mechanism other
rely upward movement occasional
occur downward create vacuum
rush forward outside say

III. Basic Hearing

The third section, *Basic Hearing*, was composed using Google
groups alerts, employing sixty-four search strings of four words
each over the course of one day from Friday, February 20 to
Saturday, February 21, 2009. The search terms were generated from
an erasure of Chapter 1, *Basic Hearing Science*, of a book entitled,
Hearing Instrument Science and Fitting Practices. Each individual
search result was first analyzed at syllable level and then arranged
by frequency of occurring syllable. As a result, each sentence of Part
I contains a unique syllable that does not appear again in the rest of
the text; each sentence of Part II contains a syllable that repeats once
in the rest of the text; and each sentence of Part III contains a syllable
that repeats twice in the rest of the text. Spacing between sentences
in each section reflects how syllable groups were gathered together
and arranged. A single hard return between groups indicates a
transition to a different organizing syllable. In each section groups
were arranged to highlight connections between other syllables
that also repeated across the groups. Consideration was given to

second, third, fourth and fifth orders of organizing syllables. Once search results were arranged the order was not modified and no result was deleted. What emerged was a highly idiosyncratic and essentially non-repeatable process. Some of the structural rigor may have been discarded in the process of editing the final text. As each search result was modified to create a single entry and in most cases a single sentence, some of the organizing syllables may have been modified or edited out of the text. All pronouns were changed to gendered third person pronouns and verb tenses were shifted, though some first and second person pronouns were allowed if they could be interpellated into the third person perspective being created throughout the text.

Basic Hearing search strings:
stimulus sensation crudely imperfectly
perceptual ability clearly limited
guessing fairly recently reliable
human hampered virtual inaccessibility

ear help old thoughts
changed interpretations oval middle
nerve internal organ external
round membrane promontory overall

blend controversy probable earlier
popular tree forest nature
listener vicinity medium air
possible dimensions aspects generation

perception relationship loudness intensity
boundary consideration impaired listeners
scale energy travel pathways
primary consists minute particles

motion random slight hardly
detect gently particularly manner
movement threshold normal average

person vibratory string voice

tuning adjacent collide identical
chain events occurs successively
original source ultimate destination
space time striking wave

alternately pressed tightly portion
further apart during parameters
describe resulting past point
cause pressure formed move

permission displaced resting related
subjective within diaphragm aid
microphone respond accurately faithfully
caused displacement expressed power

tremendous detection feeling compare
found approximately greater softest
enormous range intensities awkward
deal easily shortcut method

devised express large ratios
named simply whenever value
compared called defined values
counted refers means needed

smaller resulted origin apparent
proportional reference sense say
stated establish gain causes
increase relative result fold

results peak saturation level
choice specify hear everyday
produced systems steps previously
advantage able supplementary information

interested referred small aware
difficult beginning concept require
need review descriptions complex
made series pure tones

broken technique spectral way
representing terms phase speech
speaker characterized resonances vocal
shape production various occur

distribution inner performs entering
separates plot hearing thought
response signal simple tone
rarefaction condensation produces varies

figure vertical horizontal generated
harmonic plucked violin vibrating
common narrow blip temporal
odd overtones decreasing domain

Mathew Timmons

About The Poet

Mathew Timmons' projects include *The New Poetics, CREDIT, Where is it Written?, After Darío*, and *The Archanoids* (a CD of solo and collaborative sound poetries). His visual and performance work has been shown at Human Resources Gallery, Shoshana Wayne Gallery, Public Fiction, François Ghebaly Gallery, LACE, Museum of Contemporary Art Denver, California College of the Arts, ArtSpeak Vancouver, LACMA, and the UCLA Hammer Museum. Mathew works as the General Director of General Projects and as the editor and publisher of Insert Blanc Press in Los Angeles.

Mathew Timmons